UNDERGROUND BASES

*Subterranean Military Facilities
and the Cities Beneath Our Feet*

THE UNDERGROUND KNOWLEDGE SERIES

James&Lance
MORCAN

UNDERGROUND BASES: Subterranean Military Facilities and the Cities Beneath Our Feet

Published by:
Sterling Gate Books
78 Pacific View Rd,
Papamoa 3118,
Bay of Plenty,
New Zealand
sterlinggatebooks@gmail.com

Special Note: This title is an extended version of Chapter 19 of *The Orphan Conspiracies: 29 Conspiracy Theories from The Orphan Trilogy* (Sterling Gate Books, 2014) by James Morcan & Lance Morcan. This title therefore contains a combination of new material as well as recycled material (in many cases verbatim excerpts) from *The Orphan Conspiracies*.

National Library of New Zealand publication data:

Morcan, James 1978-
Morcan, Lance 1948-
Title: UNDERGROUND BASES: Subterranean Military Facilities and the Cities Beneath Our Feet
Edition: First ed.
Format: Paperback
Publisher: Sterling Gate Books
ISBN: 978-0-473-36540-0

CONTENTS

■■■■■■■■■■■■■■■■■■

FOREWORD

■■■■■■■■■■■■■■■■■■

BY JERRY GRIFFIN

"There's something going on. You just can't see it all," says Mr. Woodward somewhere right now in the closing lines of *The Lake Drain* science fiction film. It streams above ground online.

If the Holly Wood (used to make a magician's wand) feature film *All the President's Men* was about the reality of worldwide governmental deep underground construction then the famous line would read, "Follow the concrete" instead of "Follow the money." The source in the film (and novel) was, of course, "Deep Throat," a deep undercover (alleged) contact.

Follow the worldwide concrete production reports over the last decades (focus on the mid-

90's.) You most likely will not find evidence where that tremendous production volume was mixed with water and can now be located in governmental structures. You may see obvious evidence using a "satellite" mapping system available on the computers we are allowed to have. This would be the entrances to what James & Lance Morcan have detailed so nicely before you now (see Chapter 4, "Lockheed Martin" entrance photo).

Ever look at something and not know what you were looking at? Later, did you realize what you saw and only then you discovered...you did not know what you were looking at?

Welcome aboard. You will see from the authors' work here that underground activity has occurred way before you were born. (For intelligent questions here about being born you might look into the authors' *GENIUS INTELLIGENCE: Secret Techniques and Technologies to Increase IQ*, book one in *The Underground Knowledge Series*.) Links to all their works are at the end of this publication. You may come across why you are smart.

So, if we are smart and also not readily aware that underground life is an ancient reality then our "text" books must be front-loaded. Someone consistently keeps overwhelming evidence from our immediate reach.

Ancient cities exist below our feet right now.

Maybe way down and a little to the left depending on where you are standing or sitting.

Right now you are reading and if you were to get up and travel quite a distance, possibly, you would find the archaeological existence of great machined caverns below your feet. This means machinery of a higher technology than you might be used to up here on the surface while sitting and reading. Look up, "Subterrene Machine." You will have a blast.

Some ancient cities underground, too, were machined and one need look no further here on the surface for remaining archaeological evidence than cut stones around the Giza pyramid complex in Egypt (Khemet.) There also exists right now megalithic rock structures cut to laser-like precision (in South America for example) and massive underwater monuments and cities discovered in various parts of the world. (Example – see: Foerster, Brien, *Lost Ancient Technology of Peru and Bolivia*).

Quite possibly Lance Morcan's upcoming work titled *NEW ZEALAND*, an epic adventure novel covering 500 years of South Pacific and Polynesian history, will also uncover evidence. Megalithic construction and underground living facilities must also pepper Polynesian life. (Ever see a picture of one of the Easter Island "heads" excavated below ground to show huge standing figures?).

Mr. Woodward in my film mentioned at top is a journalist hounded by black ops machinery only to find there is no end to the layers involved in going down the "rabbit hole" or "the lake drain."

There is something behind it all and even those inside cannot see or know it all.

You might consult the Morcans' *Underground Knowledge Series I-V* to be awakened to the reality that you have been offered – a programming which skims the surface.

The great thing about running into researchers away from corporate (mental) news (programming) is when your research intersects through an ongoing process of elimination. There is always something to reassess. (Just search a moment for "Anatoly Fomenko" and you may understand to what I refer).

We are programmed by those controllers who have already been in this area of deprogramming research. See Chapter 11 here for evidence programmed right before your eyes in the Denver Airport Murals.

This is where the words "Satanic" and "Masonic" must, at least, be mentioned for an overarching perspective on who is involved in "programming." A pentagram is a pentagram is a star. A rose represents Rosicrucian and robed

Jesuits wear black for Saturn and red and white for Santa, er, Satan.

So, they are already over here in this area of underground bases and tunnels research. Here (Chapters 8 & 9) is this place you will discover in the material below called *Dulce*. The word means "sweet" in Spanish.

"Alleged" is mentioned here as he also does in my film interviews with Richard Sauder, Ph.D., an internationally noted and referenced author on the subject. The military regularly references his blog.

He says from personal conversation with the major parties concerned in Chapters 8 & 9 that "Dulce is sweet disinformation". ('Richard Sauder, Ph.D. Atop A Nuclear Silo on Deprogrammed Radio HD', approx. 1:20:00 sec.- and can be found online on Youtube. He also addresses WHY the elites would build these warrens). Much of the Alternative Media promotes and refers to Dulce Deep Underground Military Base as a fact and there exists no evidence according to this interviewed author and researcher.

Read on. Go down the warren. The Lake Drain. Come to understand these 'continuity of government' projects exist not for you but for those with the knowledge that something will be occurring, causing people to once again retreat underground.

Below, James & Lance Morcan will help you understand what you are looking at.

Jerry Griffin

Producer/Director of The Lake Drain

(thelakedrainfilm.com)

INTRODUCTION

██████████████████████

In 1998, one of us (James) took a guided tour through the Pentagon, the US Department of Defense headquarters in Arlington County, Virginia. It was quite an eye-opener.

The tour guide was a young military staffer and the other 50 or so tour party members included a chubby, garrulous boy of about eight or nine who spoke with a southern drawl and was constantly eating. Between mouthfuls of food, the boy interrupted the tour guide's running commentary in a loud voice, asking, "What about the levels below the Pentagon, sir?"

The tour guide politely but firmly replied, "Son, there are no levels below the Pentagon, what you see is all there is."

That reply seemed to satisfy the boy until about five minutes later he repeated the question and received a near identical response. This same question-same answer pattern continued for the remainder of the tour, visibly raising the young staffer's aggravation levels every time he was interrupted and forced to answer the persistent boy.

In all likelihood the boy had watched TV shows or movies referencing the conspiracy theory which insists there are miles of tunnels, subterranean levels and underground bunkers below the Pentagon, suggesting what's seen above ground is merely the tip of the iceberg.

Pure fantasy? Imagine for a moment a reality where all the technologies that futurists have predicted have already been invented and are currently being used by a privileged few.

There have been numerous reports of scientific inventions that never saw the light of day even though they were perfected and ready to go on the market. Rumors of these radical inventions date back to the post-Industrial Revolution period in the late 1800's and early 1900's, and have persisted right up to and including the present day.

Were a documentary film ever to be produced based on the conspiratorial history of suppressed technologies, the individuals featured would include everyone from inventors who either suddenly died, went missing or faded into obscurity, to tech investors who were mysteriously thwarted to scientists who lost their patents without receiving any valid explanation.

Still skeptical? Look no further than Nikola Tesla, aka the Electric Magician (1856-1943). Most secret technologies are rumored to be based on the works of this brilliant Croatian-born Serbian-American scientist, inventor, physicist and electrical engineer.

Tesla was, in the view of many, history's most underrated scientist. To comprehend what he achieved in his eventful lifetime is to believe in the possibility of the Splinter Civilization's existence, and to ultimately understand its nature.

The Electric Magician's astounding official achievements in the scientific field are too many to list here, but, for those not familiar with his life story, we encourage you to study it. (We summarize the Tesla story in *The Orphan Conspiracies*).

As revolutionary as Nikola Tesla's known inventions and experiments sound, it's his long-rumored suppressed inventions that have spawned countless theories.

If such technologies do exist, that would likely confirm there is a covert civilization – we prefer to call it a *Splinter Civilization* – that secretly and autonomously resides on our planet right now.

Such a group's membership would probably be a combination of high-ranking military personnel, senior intelligence agents as well as shadowy government figures and many of the global elite, the 1% who, through their power and influence, hold sway over the majority (the 99%). Although all citizens of various nations and speaking different languages, they would be united by the common goal of attaining mass power, or a New World Order.

Because of its almost infinite sources of funding – mostly derived from black ops appropriations – this Splinter Civilization would have in its possession technologies that would make a layman's mind boggle. The covert civilization would use inconceivable, stealth-like weaponry to wage quiet wars on vulnerable nations. Such weaponry could even facilitate alteration of the weather and the creation of so-called acts of nature.

And of course, *contractors* commissioned by faceless middlemen employed by the shadowy members of this splinter group would, one way or another, silence any investigative reporters or citizen journalists who come close to uncovering evidence of its existence.

Sounds like a theory that should be reserved for science fiction movies or novels?

You'd be right, except for one important point. Many of these suppressed technologies

Above: Was Nikola Tesla's revolutionary science suppressed or classified?

"Tesla3" by Napoleon Sarony
postcard 1890, scanned from my collection in 2007
cropped from: image:Tesla2.jpg.
Licensed under Public Domain via Wikimedia Commons

Above: A DARPA design for a secret underground facility.

"Underground facility" by DARPA
This file was derived from:
DARPA Strategic Plan (2005).pdf.
Licensed under Public Domain via Wikimedia Commons

have been reported by former engineers and other employees of the Military Industrial Complex. And the list of whistleblowers is an extensive and impressive one that dates back decades.

Based on the reports of those same whistleblowers, it appears suppression of scientific technologies is done for various reasons. Sometimes it's about governments wanting to achieve or maintain superior military might. Other times it's for financial reasons.

Few would deny it's in the interests of corporations that financially benefit from current technologies to block newer, more advanced technologies ever reaching the marketplace. Though immoral, that would make good business sense as it's an unwritten rule that corporations squash competitors and quash competition.

If you're wondering how this Splinter Civilization with all its suppressed technologies, manpower and equipment could exist without the mass public's knowledge then consider what's below the surface. Literally.

That's right folks, we're talking about the hidden *black world* beneath our feet – another favorite theory of a million-and-one diehard conspiracy theorists, but also a theory many genuine researchers believe as well.

In our international thriller series, a shadowy agency's secret headquarters are sited one mile below ground. This decision for the storyline was inspired by longstanding rumors of military bunkers and enormous underground facilities not known to the general public.

One book critic commented at the end of her review of our series as follows: "Quite thought-provoking books, too, when you ponder on what the world's super powers are really up to in their underground bunkers!"

That comment got us thinking. What the hell are the powers-that-be doing below ground and why are they building such facilities?

We refer, of course, to *secret* underground facilities as opposed to *official* underground facilities whose purpose is obvious and whose existence is common knowledge or at least officially acknowledged in records accessible to the public.

In the course of researching this particular book, we came across a number of convincing sources that appear to confirm the existence of at least some secret subterranean facilities.

Though you don't need to be Sherlock Holmes to source this information, you do need patience and time – time to connect the dots. Due to our fascination with this subject, and interrelated classified subjects, we believe we have connected the necessary dots to open your eyes to another world. A world literally beneath our feet!

Our sources, incidentally, include declassified US Government files, university reports, WikiLeaks' documents and eyewitness accounts from common citizens who have stumbled across such bases, as well as interviews with, and testimonials from, former military personnel who claim to have worked in underground bunkers.

James Morcan & Lance Morcan

1

■■■■■■■■■■■■■■■■■■■

D.U.M.B.

"According to our best estimates, more than
half of all U.S. government records are
classified. For an archivist seeking to preserve
and understand our history, that means most
of our history is kept secret from us, think
about that for a moment."

–Richard Dolan

If we are correct and a more scientifically
advanced *offshoot* of humanity (the Splinter
Civilization referred to in the introduction) co-
exists on the planet right now, it's a safe bet *they*
maintain their secrecy by going about much of
their business in underground bases. Not only
in America, but most likely the world over.

Where else short of colonizing another planet could they hide the required plant, machinery and equipment – and the manpower to operate it – away from the prying eyes of Joe Citizen, investigative journalists and inquisitive everyday people like us?

Worth noting is that security at the entrances to *known and acknowledged* underground facilities is at least equal to security at the border checkpoints that separate nations. This seems to add some weight to the theory that we are dealing with a Splinter Civilization and this small but powerful group have purposefully divided themselves from official society, or from the world as we know it. More correctly, the global elite have separated *us* from their society because they're able to operate in both worlds – above and below ground.

We accept the concept of such a breakaway group may still seem hard to fathom, but consider comments made by Daniel K. Inouye, US Senator from Hawaii, in his testimony at the 1987 Iran-Contra Hearings.

"There exists a shadowy government," Inouye said, "with its own Air Force, its own Navy, its own fundraising mechanism, and the ability to pursue its own ideas of national interest, free from all checks and balances, and free from the law itself."

Above: An underground military fortress in Switzerland.

"Fort «Furggels» - Main Tunnel Upper Level (5050187503)"
by Kecko from Switzerland (Rheintal SG,
the border valley between Switzerland and Austria)
Fort «Furggels» - Main Tunnel Upper Level
Uploaded by High Contrast.
Licensed under CC BY 2.0 via Wikimedia Commons

According to our research, this Splinter Civilization was able to grow so powerful and remain largely below the radar due to a number of complex events, which all intersected mid to late last century.

One was the apparent arrival of extra-terrestrials en masse, allegedly commencing around the time of the widely reported yet still classified Roswell UFO incident in New Mexico in 1947.

Another was the scientific improvements in tunnelling and digging technologies from the 1950's onwards. Again, one of us (Lance) can speak with a little authority on this, having gone through the Mount Isa Mines school of mining in the Outback of Queensland, Australia, working as an underground miner back in the late 1960's and following mining developments around the world with interest ever since.

The third reason was the Cold War whose 'national security' demands and the resulting unhealthy culture of secrecy it gave rise to encouraged governments to be less accountable to their citizens.

These coinciding factors all created a *perfect storm* for underground bases to be built and managed by the Military Industrial Complex and intelligence agencies as well as private corporations.

Above: Former US Secretary of the Navy Donald C. Winter (in blue) on a guided tour of an underground facility in Hawaii.

"US Navy 070823-N-3642E-319
Secretary of the Navy (SECNAV) the Honorable Dr. Donald C. Winter tours the Red Hill Underground Fuel Storage Facility to get a first-hand look at the condition of the tanks"
by U.S. Navy photo by Chief Mass Communication Specialist Shawn P. Eklund
This Image was released by the United States Navy with the ID 070823-N-3642E-319
Licensed under Public Domain via Wikimedia Commons

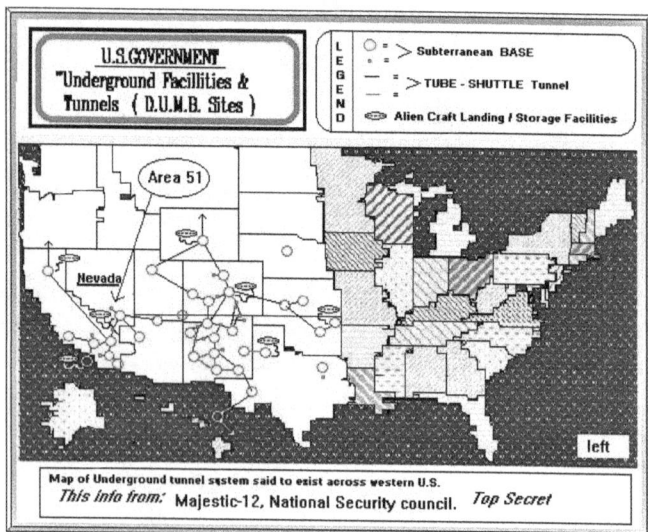

Above: Underground sites said to exist in the western USA.

(image credit: public domain)

"The covert underground infrastructure serves many functions. Among these are strategic storage of materials and weapons, clandestine research and production facilities, alternant basing for military personnel and equipment, surface environment control systems (atmospheric lensing, synthetic earthquakes, weather modification, civilian population control, etc)."

–Dr. Steven J. Smith. Excerpt from the paper
Underground Infrastructure –
The missing forty trillion dollars.

Those who have researched unacknowledged subterranean facilities are almost unanimous in their belief that the bases are funded by black budgets financed by a combination of banksters, drug wars and profits from (mainly mineral) resources plundered from unwitting Third World countries.

The US program for building these underground bunkers is known as DUMB, or Deep Underground Military Bases. DUMB has apparently been in operation since the late 1940's and there are now said to be hundreds of such bases in almost every state in mainland America.

"Two baseline questions regarding whether or not DUMBs actually exist: Do the elite command the technology to create underground cities connected by supersonic Maglev trains? Are the elite psychopathic enough to intentionally disrupt Earth's life-support system?"

−Veterans Today, February 10, 2013 article Elite Underground.

2

∎∎∎∎∎∎∎∎∎∎∎∎∎∎∎∎∎∎∎∎

THE PENTAGON AND THE WHITEHOUSE

"Underground DUMBs connected by supersonic train systems are a tender topic for the elite. So their mainstream corporate media (MSM) buries DUMBs and the supporting black-operations (Black-Ops) budget. Never a peep."

–Veterans Today, February 10, 2013 article Elite Underground.

In the 21st Century, it's basically common knowledge and certainly widely accepted that the Pentagon has multiple levels of enormous bunkers and an immense network of tunnels beneath its visible exterior.

It makes complete sense, too. You'd expect the Department of Defense's headquarters of the world's greatest superpower would have multiple access routes and escape tunnels to accommodate sudden evacuations and other emergency actions.

For an overview of the Pentagon's *official* history and specifications, *History.com* is hard to beat. Excerpts follow from a January 15, 2013 article by author Barbara Maranzani published on the site:

"On January 15, 1943, work was completed on the new headquarters for the U.S. War Department...in Arlington, Virginia. The massive complex, commonly known as the Pentagon, was built to house the nearly 30,000 defense workers tasked with helping America win World War II. With more than 17 miles of corridors, it remains one of the largest office buildings in the world, and has become a symbol—for better and for worse—of military might."

Ms Maranzani then lists a series of little known facts about the Pentagon. The following are some of the more interesting:

"One of (Brigadier General Brehorn) Somervell's first dictates was that the massive

Above: What lies beneath The Pentagon?

"The Pentagon January 2008"
by David B. Gleason from Chicago, IL - The Pentagon.
Licensed under CC BY-SA 2.0 via Wikimedia Commons

Above: Pentagon staff fled to "undisclosed underground facility" on 9/11?

"DF-SD-02-09094" by TSGT JIM VARHEGYI, USAF - [1].
Licensed under Public Domain via Wikimedia Commons

building be no taller than five stories (plus two stories below ground). This was due, in part, to...a more practical reason—the steel shortage already underway in a nation girding for war. Instead of steel, the building was built primarily of reinforced concrete, 435,000 cubic yards of it...

"It's pretty difficult to understand just how big the Pentagon is. In fact, the U.S. Capitol could fit into just one of the building's five sides, and with 5,100,000 square feet, it has twice the office space of the Empire State Building."

The author concludes that in the wake of 9/11, "when American Airlines Flight 77 smashed into the building's east side... plans were soon underway for an extensive reconstruction program, dubbed the Phoenix Project, which was completed in February 2003 at a cost of $5 billion—five times the cost of the original building."

As an interesting aside, Ms Maranzani reveals that the same person oversaw both the Pentagon's construction and the Manhattan Project, the initiative that resulted in the development of the world's first atomic bomb. She writes, "While Somervell was officially in charge of the Pentagon project, it fell to...Major Leslie Groves, to make it a reality...While still working on the Pentagon, Groves was also put in charge of the Manhattan Project" and "was involved in nearly every aspect of the top-secret project, selecting and constructing clandestine sites for the research facilities and its workers across the country."

That's the official account of the Pentagon and its construction specifications and history.

However, it's the unofficial story we are interested in.

In an article dated June 23, 2008, commentator/blogger Steve Warran states: "There always was something fishy about the Pentagon ground-floor deck slab following the attack of 9-11; where evidently, a 757-jetliner was flown absolutely level into the first floor of the building without so much as nicking the poured concrete foundation. Even after journeying 300 feet in, with enough explosive energy to punch holes through thick masonry walls (while also deflecting the second-floor slab upward along the way,) the deck was left immaculate enough to roller skate on."

More to the point, Warran thanks military historian, Barbara Honegger, for "clearing up the space-planning mystery at least". He refers to the article Ms Honegger published in September 2006 titled, *The Pentagon Attack Papers: Seven Hours in September: The Clocks that Broke the Lie,* in which "she informs us of a previously undisclosed underground facility".

Above: Representative Gerald R. Ford beneath the Capitol Building.

*"Photograph of Representative Gerald R. Ford
Walking Through the Tunnels Beneath the
United States Capitol Building - NARA - 186884"
Gerald R. Ford Presidential Library: H0012-1.
Licensed under Public Domain via Wikimedia Commons –*

It's a similar situation in Washington D.C. where it has been widely reported by mainstream media that there's a vast tunnel system below the capital. And it's our understanding that at any given time there are hundreds of security personnel patrolling the tunnels, on foot or with the aid of motorized vehicles.

Very likely many of D.C.'s tunnels lead to and from the White House. The often-told stories of Marilyn Monroe being sneaked in and out of the White House via underground tunnels to meet with JFK would seem to confirm this. Such tales reveal the capital's extensive tunnel system enabled Marilyn to be the President's mistress without much scandal – for a period, at least.

In an article dated April 4, 2011, the UK's *Daily Mail* asks if "a secret lair was being built under the White House".

The *Daily Mail* article continues: "The West Wing of the White House is all-but disappearing behind an $86 million building project that is going to last for years. And a mysterious tunnel is being built, fuelling speculation that a secret underground lair is what's really under construction.

"In recent weeks, an expanding and sometimes ear-splitting zone of excavation has enveloped the mansion's famous office wing...

"The White House already has a number of tunnels —the exact number is, of course, classified.

"The most well known is the underground corridor that leads to the President's Emergency Operations Center (PEOC), a supposedly nuclear-proof bunker located six stories under the East Wing. It was to this bunker and its adjacent Executive Briefing Room that Dick Cheney and Condoleezza Rice, among others, directed Government operations on September 11, 2001.

"While Hollywood and many conspiracy theorists suggest a rabbit warren of subterranean passageways— including mythical tunnels to Capitol Hill and even Camp David —there is at least one hidden passageway that has been revealed in the famous residence."

The *Daily Mail* confirms "a 50-yard tunnel leads from a concealed doorway in the Oval Office to the basement of the First Family's residence" in the East Wing.

"The clandestine passage was built during Ronald Reagan's presidency as a way to guard the President in a terrorist attack...Pressing a panel on a wall adjacent to the President's rest room next to the Oval Office causes a secret door to slide open, leading to a staircase down to the passageway."

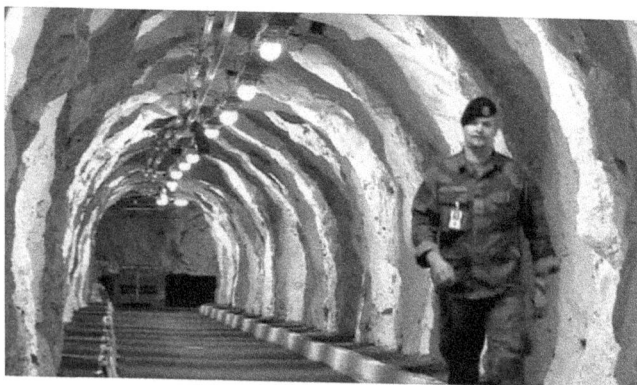

Above: A soldier in an unknown underground base.

(photo credit: public domain)

The *Daily Mail* also asserts there is talk of a tunnel linking the White House to Blair House across Pennsylvania Avenue.

Before It's News columnist Monica Davis, in an article dated February 20, 2013, says "the massive 4 year White House construction project has finally been completed." She's referring to the same "secret lair" the *Daily Mail* reported on earlier.

Excerpts from Ms Davis' article follow:

"The deep, underground project continues to be shrouded in secrecy and has reportedly been planned for 40 years...

"Given that the president has so many fortified hidey holes, why was this one built? What does its construction really mean for the security of the most powerful man in the world?

"...And deep underground, whatever has been built there remains shrouded in mystery."

3

■■■■■■■■■■■■■■■■■

UNDERGROUND CITIES

"Civilians are involved, obviously. Because there are medical and scientific personnel. A woman who was working at a university hospital, a big one in Arkansas, was wanting to move, get a better job. She was in the office computer end of things, not the medical end. She got an offer; apparently a real smart woman and good at her job. She got a phone call, having gone to a "head hunter" for different job possibilities in (various) areas; got a call back for an interview with an astounding salary base. But she had to fly to Dallas to be interviewed, and they paid for her flight to Dallas. She met at a restaurant with representatives of this company. And they told her almost nothing; very, very little about the details of the work. (I think it frightened her quite a bit after she thought about it.) But it was great pay. They said they would pay for her to relocate. The one question they asked that made it stop for her was: The job, by the way, was underground. You would have to be underground for two years. You could not come up for two years – not that you'd work underground, then go home on the surface. You'd have to stay underground and live and work for two years if you want the job – pays a lot of money, gives you a lot of benefits. But you stay underground."

–Dr. Karla Turner, from an interview in a 1995 issue of Paranoia magazine.

By all appearances, the US Government is building underground cities in preparation for a coming catastrophe they seem certain is imminent. Whether the elite believe it will be some kind of nuclear apocalypse or a religious, Armageddon-type scenario, nobody knows. At least, nobody we know knows.

In episode 4 of the third TV season of *Conspiracy Theory with Jesse Ventura*, former

Minnesota Governor Ventura and his son Tyrel Ventura, along with Sean Stone, son of Oscar-winning filmmaker Oliver Stone, travel to the Ozarks, a mountainous region of the central United States, to investigate rumors of underground developments there. They find the entrance to what appears to be an underground city being built inside a mountain.

Despite heavy fortifications – and no doubt aided by Ventura's status as former Governor of Minnesota – the team gain vehicular entry to the massive underground facility, which they discover covers an area of 50 square miles! As they drive around freely, they quickly deduce it is indeed an underground city in the making, complete with offices, warehouses, manufacturing plants, indoor farming facilities as well as stockpiles of food, water and crude oil.

"It's like they've got door-to-door transportation for the chosen few when it's time to move inside and weld those doors shut. I don't necessarily think it'd be a good place to live, but it would be a good place to survive."

–Jesse Ventura, from episode 4, season 3, of Conspiracy Theory with Jesse Ventura.

In an item dated November 27, 2012, Missouri television news channel KY3 reported that "According to multiple contentions made . . . on a cable television show, the Ozarks is about to become the center of what remains of human civilization."

The show it referred to is *Conspiracy Theory*.

KY3's report continues: "Mountain View, Arkansas was also featured in the production. The town's "suspiciously large number" of banks was said to be serving as the repository of the wealth of those about to move to the Ozarks to survive the end of the world. An unusually large increase in the number of earthquakes was suspicioned to be the result of the construction of underground bunkers."

The channel's report, however, debunks Governor Ventura's findings in the TV episode. You can draw your own conclusions.

One Missouri commentator reports, "The large underground structure being built just south of Springfield is said to be a private residence constructed for a billionaire corporate bigwig which will also serve as his corporate retreat/headquarters... There's another underground storage facility in Branson, Missouri, a half hour from me. When you're driving up the highway, off to your left you see a gravel parking lot and loading docks cut into the

Above: Governor Jesse Ventura believes in underground cities.

Above: Inside a mysterious underground facility in the Ozarks.

(photo credit: public domain)

side of the cliff, several bays, going back into the mountain."

The facility this commentator refers to is Pensmore, which, officially at least, is a mansion currently under construction in the Ozarks. According to *Wikipedia*, "When completed, the home will be the private residence of Steven T. Huff and his family" and "will be one of the largest private single-family residences in the United States."

Huff, incidentally, is the chairman of TF Concrete Forming Systems, which is doing the concrete construction work for the home. Huff previously worked in Army intelligence and was a CIA officer. A company he founded produced software for, among other things, intelligence and defense applications.

According to *Wikipedia*, "The home is unique, as it is an insulated concrete form structure that is designed to showcase sustainable construction techniques on a large scale. The home is designed to be earthquake resistant, bullet proof, blast proof, tornado resistant, bug resistant, and fire resistant."

It's worth noting some hardcore conspiracy theorists believe Pensmore will serve as the new White House "from which the Illuminati will rule the US!"

That aside, it's worth asking the question: Why are so many billionaires privately building all these underground bunkers of late?

The same commentator who drew our attention to Pensmore alludes to the idea that the global elite may know of, or at least *think* they know of, a looming apocalyptic future. "I know that preppers come in all shapes and sizes and tax brackets, but even more than having the same fears and anxieties we all share at times combined with the financial wherewithal to actually do something substantial about it, perhaps they also are better informed than many of us. They might know what's coming before it does, or are playing the odds, just in case."

4

■■■■■■■■■■■■■■■■■■■

POLLING THE UNDERGROUND

There are tunnels and base complexes that connect China Lake, California City, Norton AFB, Edwards AFB, Tonopah, Groom Lake, Nevada Test Site, Los Alamos, Dulce, Norad, Oklahoma and to the East."

–John Lear, from a 2003 interview with Art Bell on the Coast to Coast radio show.

In 2014, we founded a discussion group on *Goodreads.com*, the popular literary site for readers and authors. Called *Underground Knowledge*, the group was established to encourage dialogue about underreported issues of our time.

We recently ran a poll on the subject of underground cities, asking fellow 'Undergrounders' (group members) to vote on this question: *Do you believe there are secret/classified underground cities around the world?*

During the voting period, a lively discussion unfolded in the comments below the poll's results. Some of these comments are included here. Before you read them, we must point out that the worldwide membership of the Underground Knowledge group is comprised of a diverse bunch of intelligent and revolutionary thinkers, and spans the political spectrum from the Left to the Right, or from Liberal to Conservative and virtually every political persuasion in between.

Fellow Undergrounders include *New York Times* bestselling authors, internationally-renowned scientists, leading investigative journalists, economists, social activists and whistleblowers, doctors, former intelligence agents (CIA/NSA/MI6/MOSSAD), ex-military officers and former NASA engineers. There are even Pulitzer Prize nominees.

Anyway, on the subject of whether there are actually underground cities (as opposed to the already confirmed/declassified underground bases), here are their comments:

Member 1: "It seems kinda far-fetched but with all that technology that has empowered us I do think it is highly likely."

Member 2: "Bases yes, cities no."

Member 3: "It's not impossible."

Member 4: "I believe that there are underground cities all over the world constructed in ancient times before our civilization. In Japan, we have a legend that there exists an underground city under Mt. Minakami, which has been rumored to be the ancient pyramid. In this place, we can see UFOs and strange lights at the present time. I think there are other underground cities both in North and South America. Some of them were constructed by the United States of America for some purposes."

Member 5: "My opinion is not based on any altruistic notions. I just don't think it could be kept secret in these days."

Member 6: "I don't see why not... Look at some of the underground facilities and cities of bygone eras we have found, usually by accident. Such a thing is not unbelievable with modern technology."

Member 7: "Bunkers and bases YES. From places like North Korea to Washington D.C. Paris, Rome and many others there exists extensive underground facilities. However, they're all a hodgepodge of antiquated catacombs, private bunkers, or smaller constructions. Cities? NO. No government is competent enough to hide any population larger than a few thousand, more medium company or village sized."

Member 8: "I put unsure about cities; but there are bunkers and bases used by politicians, military and civilians for safety in case of war or major disasters."

Member 9: "Definitely and I think the President is very aware of this fact. Hmm...maybe there are some bunkers in area 51. You never know...."

Member 10: "What exactly are we using as the defining perimeters of a 'city'? Wikipedia (that horrible, horrible site! lol) describes a city as "A city is a large and permanent human settlement. Although there is no agreement on how a city is distinguished from a town in general English language meanings, many cities have a particular administrative, legal, or historical status based on local law." So, based on that, "*few were larger than any nearby village*" could still be a city, and we're just splitting hairs..."

Member 11: "Not just underground but under the sea as well."

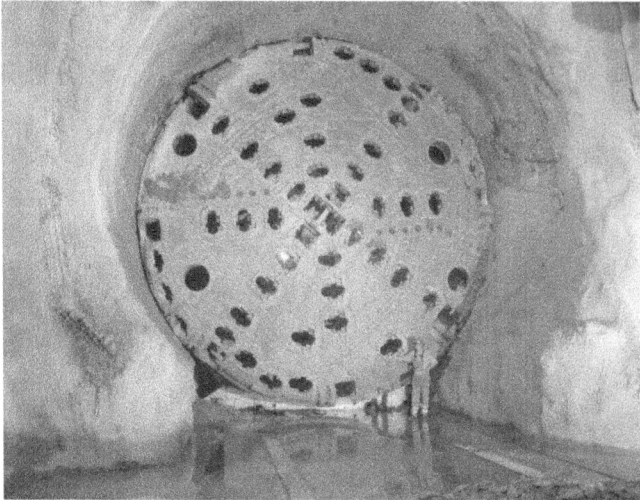

Above: Tunnel boring machine used to excavate Swiss underground base tunnel.

"TBM S-210 Alptransit Faido East"
by Cooper.ch 16:58, 19 September 2006 (UTC) - Own work.
Licensed under CC BY-SA 2.5 via Commons

Above: A Lockheed Martin private facility in California...

Is that an entrance to an underground site?

(photo credit: public domain)

Member 12: "I will support by saying this...I have done zero research on the topic nor do I have any standing knowledge of the subject. That being said, I would not be surprised one little bit if there were both ancient and modern cities beneath cities. I have personally seen one vast network under Luxembourg city, only about 1/10 was open to the public. Isn't the city under London supposed to be like Swiss cheese - with the tube and under ground labyrinthian tunnels? Who knows."

Member 13: "Military compounds for sure."

Member 14: "From Area 51 there are underground roads leading across the USA with underground petrol/diesel stations, regular sleeping hostels, medical facilities."

Member 15: "I believe there are underground cities that are secret/classified because they are the most essential places to operate in military purposes or other government related purposes."

The final result of our Underground Knowledge group poll was as follows:

- 64% of members voted YES *there are secret/classified underground cities*

- 20% of members voted UNSURE

- 16% of members voted NO

"Imagine a machine tunneling seven miles per day through solid rock, boulders and clay…virtually anything below the waterline. A machine whose heart is a compact nuclear reactor circulating liquid lithium at 2,000 degrees F. through a rotating face that melts a tunnel 40 feet in diameter; even injecting magma into fractures in bedrock for extreme solidity, sealing the tunnel with a glassy lining, and leaving no excavated material behind. Imagine a subterrene. The nuclear subterrene was born at Los Alamos National Laboratory in New Mexico. Patents were taken out in the 70s. And since their mission is a menace to public interest, subterrenes have been minimized from public awareness. It might be safe to say that subterrenes are the hottest tool going, underground. A kind of nuclear nightcrawler."

–Veterans Today, February 10, 2013 article Elite Underground.

5

██████████████████

WHAT GOES ON BENEATH THE SURFACE?

"My first exposure to this was when my husband was kidnapped by "military" before I was ever into research ... In November 1988, my husband was taken to an underground facility; completely military, completely human. He had been in the military nine years prior (to our marriage). This was very clearly, to him, a military installation and a massive storage installation. We thought (it may have been) the FEMA center in town, where we lived. Because it's the Continuity of Government FEMA facility, for one thing. And there are

> many generators/dynamos, all sorts of
> supplies. He saw this storage (type) area
> when being taken from the holding area.
> There were a number of other people in a
> very dazed, zombie–like state, as he was."
>
> *–Dr. Karla Turner, from an interview in a 1995 issue*
> *of Paranoia magazine.*

There's a long list of claims regarding the nefarious activities conducted by the global elite and their *pawns* in these underground bases. Some say they have clandestine prisons where officially designated *missing persons* and others who have dropped off the grid are held captive; some believe human-alien joint ventures are taking place in these bases to further black technologies or to advance certain species.

When it comes to suppressed science, the hit sci-fi television series *Warehouse 13*, which aired for five seasons until mid-2014, probably best portrays the secret science bunker concept. The basic plot has two US Secret Service Agents assigned to a top-secret government warehouse to protect scientific discoveries and radical technologies invented by Nikola Tesla and others – none of which the public are aware. The premise of a largely underground warehouse storing suppressed discoveries and inventions is based on conspiracy theories that have been swirling around for decades.

Surprisingly, these wild conspiracy theories are not wholly unsubstantiated. There have also been some reports from former military engineers and government geologists about supersonic transportation systems underground. Who knows, maybe the global elite travel between cities and countries below ground, utilizing the underworld's rumored faster transportation methods?

"The other guy also said there was scuttlebutt of an underground rail system that ran under the FEMA facility. Just as he said that, we felt a low rumbling beneath our feet like a subway. We noticed some suits coming in our direction and headed off."

–David Icke, Human Race Get Off Your Knees: The Lion Sleeps No More

It has also been claimed that radical biological experiments take place in the Splinter Civilization's underworld. The kind that the laws of the land above ground don't allow – such as unsanctioned forms of genetic engineering, human cloning and illegal drug testing by pharmaceutical corporations.

Some conspiracy theorists who believe complex viruses like HIV/AIDS, SARS and Ebola are all manmade, have even theorized that these viruses are manufactured and tested in underground facilities before being unleashed above ground.

"Dr. Michael E. Salla, initiator of "exopolitics" and author of a book entitled *EXPOSING U.S. GOVERNMENT POLICIES ON EXTRATERRESTRIAL LIFE* expressed his belief that there is a joint US/alien underground bio-lab beneath the Archuleta Mesa and that this must be addressed as a serious human rights abuse issue."

–Norio Hayakawa, official report of the Dulce Base Conference of 2009 in New Mexico.

Nazi-spawned technologies are also said to exist below ground. This apparently dates back to the Project Paperclip scientists who were secretly ushered in to America immediately after WW2. Project Paperclip, of course, was that US Government-sanctioned initiative (documented and on the record) that saw

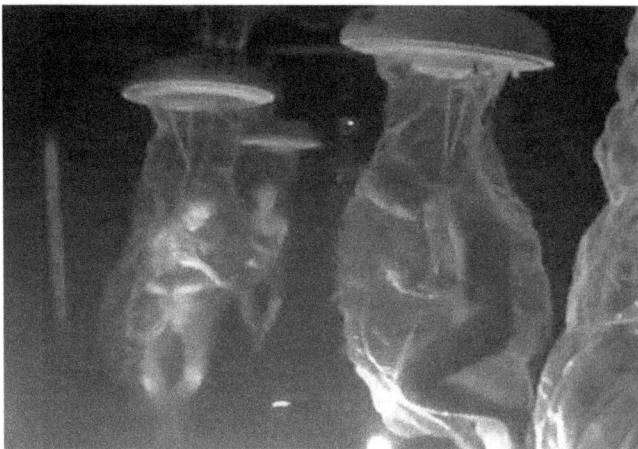

Above: An image supposedly smuggled out of Dulce Base, NM.

(photo credit: public domain)

Above: A group of 104 German Rocket scientists in Texas.

"Project Paperclip Team at Fort Bliss"
Image by NASA under Photo ID: NIX MSFC-8915531
Licensed under Public Domain via Wikimedia Commons

Werner von Braun, the German-turned naturalized American and Godfather of NASA's space rocket program, is one that many researchers have named in relation to underground bases. These Nazi Paperclip scientists were supposedly crucial to the development and construction of the underground bases and tunnels that now exist beneath American soil.

If that sounds farfetched, remember it's well-documented that von Braun and other Paperclip Nazis built V2 rockets for Hitler in large underground missile facilities in their German homeland in the 1940's.

Wildest of all, are the numerous conspiracy theories that maintain many of these underground bases – of which there are rumored to be thousands worldwide – are full of captive men, women and children.

Some suggest the captives may have been *taken* from above ground, which may partially account for the hundreds of thousands of missing persons reported annually around the world who are never found; others suggest the captives are human clones designed to spend their lives enslaved underground to further the global elite's agendas; and still others suggest some captives are used as human guinea pigs in radical science experiments conducted by scientists working for the Splinter Civilization.

And then there's the intriguing statements made by one Philip Schneider, an American geologist who, until his untimely death, also claimed to be an ex-government military engineer. Schneider said while he was involved in constructing additional bunkers in one underground base in New Mexico, he discovered aliens conducted horrific experiments on people detained in bunkers miles below the earth's surface. (More about him later).

We have no strong opinion either way as to whether aliens are with us or even if they exist. All we are doing is repeating the conspiracy theories out there concerning underground bases.

It just so happens a lot of rumors and reports – some reliable, some not – on such bases involve either aliens or alien technologies. In many instances, the theories surrounding underground bunkers and aliens cannot be separated.

6

██████████████████

COMBINING TECHNOLOGY AND MOTHER NATURE

"It is the most well kept 'secret' of all time! The earth is a much grander, mysterious and wondrous place than anyone could ever imagine in our wildest dreams! If true, an entire 'second' earth exists right below our feet! Not just in the US but nearly every point on this earth hosts an entire network of caverns of vast size and depth; honey-combed thru out the planet! There is a vast and deep underground world where advanced technology can be used freely. Where people can escape to and where all manner of *secrets* can be kept. Some very important testimonies and documents are available from certain 'military' sources (confirming) that this is real!"

—ArraiEl (Yahoo member), published on the Yahoo Voices website on 25 October 2011 in an article titled Deep Cavern Systems Worldwide.

While the vast majority of underground bases are said to have been constructed by the Military Industrial Complex, it seems most are also built inside or directly above natural, pre-existing cave networks. Either that or the constructors have made use of miles of abandoned mine tunnels and shafts.

This would make sense as those who design and build such bases would naturally look to utilize the best of nature and man – and *possibly* extra-terrestrial civilizations as well.

When it comes to American underground bases, this may not be as crazy as it first seems as much of mainland America is dotted with sinkholes, abandoned mines and enormous caves and cavern networks.

The word *cave* usually conjures up images of small caverns or fissures in the ground. But the reality is there are giant underground caves extending many, many miles underground. Some are said to be *bottomless* – and who are

Above: A lake inside the Reed Flute Cave in Guilin, China.

"Reed flute cave" by Dariusz Jemielniak - Own work.
Licensed under CC BY-SA 3.0 via Wikimedia Commons

Above: A miles-deep cave of the ancient Mayans in Belize.

"Cave in Belize" by Canon in 2D from US
Knocking at Heaven's Door.
Licensed under CC BY 2.0 via Wikimedia Commons

we to argue? For all we know, a cave or cave system could start in the wilds of Montana and end in Alaska.

Many caves, including one nicknamed the *Subterranean Grand Canyon*, are so vast only their entrances have been explored, while others – it's universally agreed – have yet to be discovered let alone explored. And many of these giant cave systems contain rare rock formations and unusual geology, significant underground rivers, lakes and seas with unique species of *cavefish* in them, as well as abundances of gemstones, crystals and gold.

The *Er Wang Dong* cave system, in China, even has its own climate system complete with clouds and rain!

On October 2, 2013, the *Daily Mail* reported, "Adventurers have stumbled across a cave so enormous that it has its own weather system, complete with wispy clouds and lingering fog inside vast caverns."

The report continues, "A team of expert cavers and photographers have been exploring the vast cave system in the Chongquing province of China and have taken the first-ever photographs of the natural wonder.

"They were amazed to discover the entrance to the hidden Er Wang Dong cave system and were stunned when they managed to climb inside to see a space so large that it can contain a cloud... The cave system discovered is not the only one with clouds inside, as humidity rises inside the caverns into colder air to form clouds inside the giant, enclosed spaces.

"The network, includes 'Cloud Ladder Hall' which itself measures around 51,000 metres squared, while there are rivers and vegetation on the floor of some of its huge caverns."

One example of the scale of underground cave systems is the extensive system known as *Craighead Caverns*, in Sweetwater, Tennessee. According to *Wikipedia*, Craighead Caverns are "best known for containing the United States' largest and the world's second largest non-subglacial underground lake, *The Lost Sea*. In addition to the lake, the caverns contain an abundance of crystal clusters called anthodites, stalactites and stalagmites, plus a waterfall."

Seen Magazine, of America's Southeast Education Network, claims Craighead Caverns was named after an Indian chief who at one time owned the property and the cave, and who may well have discovered the tiny opening that was its natural entrance.

In an article dated November 19, 2010, *Seen Magazine* reports, "During the Civil War (1863) parts of the cave were mined for salt-peter — which was used as a principal ingredient in the manufacturing of gunpowder.

"In 1905 Mr. Ben F. Sands, then just a boy...pushed beyond the fluctuating pool of the Spring Room through the tiny mud crawlway — and into the Lake Room — discovering the Lost Sea. Rumors of a large lake in Craighead Caverns had existed before Ben Sands discovery, but these may have referred to the elusive back-waters in the Spring Room, and not the actual chamber of the Lost Sea.

"In 1927 Craighead Caverns was formed. A larger more accessible entrance was opened below the natural one to make entering the cave less strenuous. The Tennessee Power Co. installed the first lighting system — which was among the first cave systems in the country."

The Lechuguilla Cave, in New Mexico, is another example of the scale of underground cave systems. Only officially discovered in 1986, Lechuguilla is the deepest cave in the US and the seventh-longest *explored* cave in the world.

According to *ExtremeScience.com*, this cave is a winding, twisting underground maze which has yet to be completely explored and mapped. Currently, 101 miles of Lechuguilla have been explored and mapped, with no end in sight. So far, the deepest part of the cave measured goes down 1,632 feet.

This almost pales to insignificance when compared to the deepest cave in the world – identified by *ExtremeScience.com* as Voronja, or "Crow's Cave", in the western Caucasus Mountains of the Georgian Republic, which "has officially been verified to be 7,021 feet deep." According to *Wikipedia*, it remains the only known cave on Earth deeper than 2,000 meters or one and a quarter miles.

Given the scale of these naturally-occurring subterranean cavities, perhaps the theory of building in, around or on top of such geological systems when constructing underground bases would not only seem prudent, but practical.

It's also worth noting that access to many of the world's largest caves, including the Lechuguilla Cave, is restricted to approved scientific researchers and government employees. This fact may dovetail with the conspiracy theory that says some of the largest caves are either controlled by the government or lie below completely restricted lands like Nevada's Area 51, for example.

Then again, we concede that denying public access to such caves could simply be a matter of safety or conservation concerns, or both.

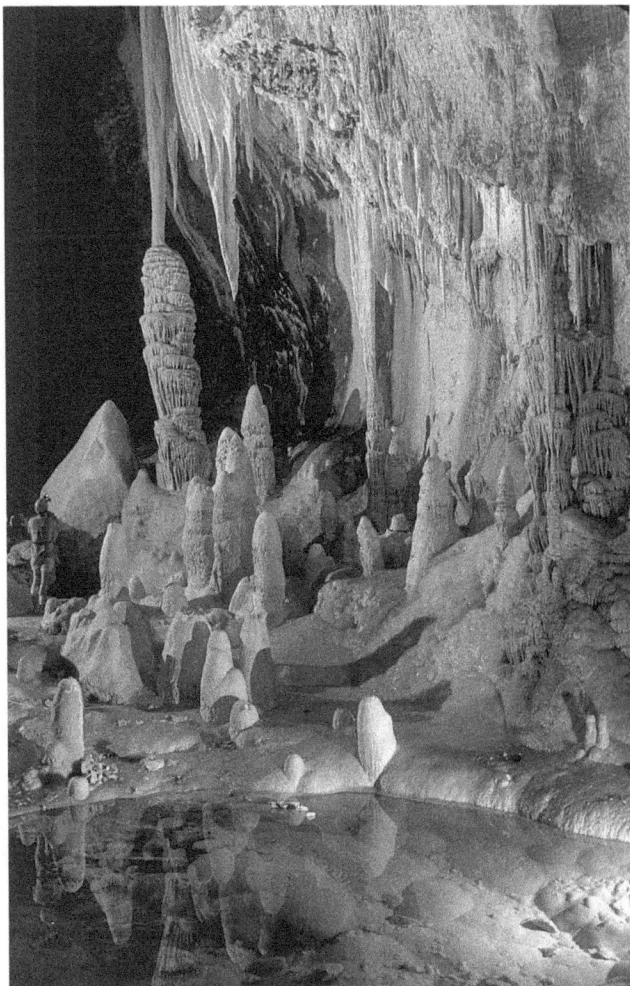

Above: The Pearlsian Gulf in the Lechuguilla Cave.

"Lechuguilla Cave Pearlsian Gulf" by Dave Bunnell
Licensed under CC BY-SA 2.5 via Wikimedia Commons

7

■■■■■■■■■■■■■■■■■■

MOUNT WEATHER

"They're doing some pretty scary things up
on the Mountain."

*–Quote from a source of a 2001 Washington Post
article on the government relocation site, Mount Weather.*

An hour's drive from Washington D.C. is
Mount Weather, a massive underground
complex in the state of Virginia. It's basically a
military base within a hollowed-out mountain.

As UK newspaper *The Guardian* reports in
an article dated August 28, 2006, the
underground emergency operations facility was
"originally built to house governmental officials
in the event of a full-scale nuclear exchange".

However, with the Cold War over, the article goes on to speculate that "as the Bush administration wages its war on terror, Mount Weather is believed to house a 'shadow government' made up of senior Washington officials on temporary assignment".

Officially at least, the Mount Weather Emergency Operations Center is a civilian command facility used as the center of operations for FEMA, the Federal Emergency Management Agency, which, in itself, has attracted more than its share of controversy.

> **"I'll be glad to tell you all about it, but I'd have to kill you afterward."**
>
> *–Bob Blair, FEMA spokesman, in response to questions about Mount Weather by investigative reporter, Ted Gup, in 1991.*

Although a major relocation site for high level officials, no outsiders have ever been allowed inside Mount Weather.

However, Richard Pollock, an author and a regular contributor for *Progressive Magazine*, interviewed several individuals who claimed to

Above: An aerial view of Mount Weather's above ground area.

"FEMA - 35049 - VA MWEOC" by Karen Nutini
This image is from the FEMA Photo Library.
Licensed under Public Domain via Wikimedia Commons

have previously been employed on site within the mountain.

The interviewees said the base had its own lake with fresh spring water, independent power generation, cafeterias, hydroponic gardens, hospitals and transportation system as well as residential apartments. They also said Mount Weather has its own fire and police departments and, as you can no doubt imagine, its own laws too.

Taking the speculation about a shadow government in *The Guardian* article one step further, Pollock reported the underground facility has its own replica government, which apparently is every bit as comprehensive as the official government above ground.

According to *Wikipedia*, "Both Mount Weather and The Greenbrier, a hotel resort and site of a massive underground bunker in Greenbriar County, West Virginia, were featured in the A&E documentary *Bunkers*.

"The documentary, first broadcast on October 23, 2001, features extensive interviews with engineers and political and intelligence analysts, providing rare insights into the secret installations...(It) compared The Greenbrier and Mount Weather to Saddam Hussein's control bunker buried beneath Bagdhad."

The Greenbriar, incidentally, was code-named *Project Greek Island* and was intended as an emergency shelter for members of the US Congress during the Cold War although it appears it was never used for its intended purpose.

"It's (Mount Weather) kind of mind-boggling. Dr. Strangelove is one of my favorite movies, and you can fantasize about that site in similar ways. It's otherworldly—just the size and weight and massiveness of the doors. It's a mini-city—like a space station."

–Buford Macklin, former emergency coordinator of the Department of Housing and Urban Development.

8

■■■■■■■■■■■■■■■■■■■

THE ALLEGED DULCE BASE

"Hayakawa several times alluded to an allegation that the government, beginning in the early 1970s and lasting till the early 1980s, may have conducted clandestine operations in the area involving experiments with bovine diseases, anthrax and other substances as part of biological warfare research. He also alluded to another allegation that there may also have been some illegal dumping or storage of toxic chemicals and other bio-hazardous materials in the nearby areas."

–Norio Hayakawa, official report of the Dulce Base Conference of 2009 in New Mexico.

One of the most commonly referred to sites mentioned by underground base researchers is an unconfirmed one said to exist below the small and almost entirely Native American-populated town of Dulce, in New Mexico.

There are many stories of government collaborations with aliens in *Dulce Base* where all manner of exotic research is apparently conducted within its seven or more vast subterranean levels and numerous tunnel offshoots. By all accounts this includes advanced mind control and psychotronic warfare experiments as well as genetic engineering.

Some Dulce researchers believe levels 5 and below are occupied entirely by alien personnel and house technologies also alien to this planet. The deepest sections of the underground base are apparently connected to an extensive cave system, which as we've mentioned seems to be common theme for most underground bases.

Dulce is believed to have interconnected bases in New Mexico, including the rumored ones at Sandia Base and White Sands, with tunnel systems linking them all. Perhaps tellingly, part of the aforementioned almost 140 mile-long and still not fully discovered cavern system known as the Lechuguilla Cave is said by some to extend all the way to some of the other bases Dulce connects to.

"Dulce is a small town in northern New Mexico, located above 7,000 feet on the Jicarilla Apache Indian Reservation. There is only one major motel and a few stores. It's not a resort town and it is not bustling with activity. But Dulce has a deep, dark secret. The secret is harbored deep below the brush of Archuleta Mesa. Function: Research of mind related functions, genetic experiments, mind control training and reprograming ... There are over 3000 real-time video cameras throughout the complex at high-security locations (entrances and exits). There are over 100 secret exits near and around Dulce. Many around Archuleta Mesa, others to the south around Dulce Lake and even as far east as Lindrith ... Deep sections of the complex connect into natural cavern systems."

–*North Star Report,* DEEP UNDERGROUND MILITARY BASES IN AMERICA.

Dulce Base first came to the public's attention in 1979 when New Mexico businessman Paul Bennowitz was convinced he had intercepted communications between antigravity flying machines and underground installations in the area.

In the 1980's, when Bennowitz claimed he'd discovered the Dulce Base, the story spread like wildfire in conspiracy circles and the UFO community in particular.

In the 1990's, US commercial airline pilot John Lear, the son of *Lear Jet* designer William P. Lear, also claimed he had confirmed the existence of Dulce Base, *independently* of Bennowitz. However, this is tempered by the writings of political scientist Michael Barkun. The professor emeritus of political science at New York's Syracuse University believes that Cold War underground missile installations in New Mexico falsely excited ufologists and conspiracy theorists.

In Barkun's opinion there's nothing else there to support rumors of an underground base at Dulce or rumors of supposed human-alien collaborations.

However, many Dulce locals, as well as quite a few independent researchers, continue to maintain there is a large site beneath the town.

Norio Hayakawa, a New Mexico resident who has independently studied Dulce Base for decades, wrote an article dated March 28, 2007 on the *Rense.com* website, which detailed his extensive research into the Dulce rumors over the years.

Above: An image supposedly smuggled out of Dulce Base

by Thomas Costello (now missing & presumed dead).
(photo credit: public domain)

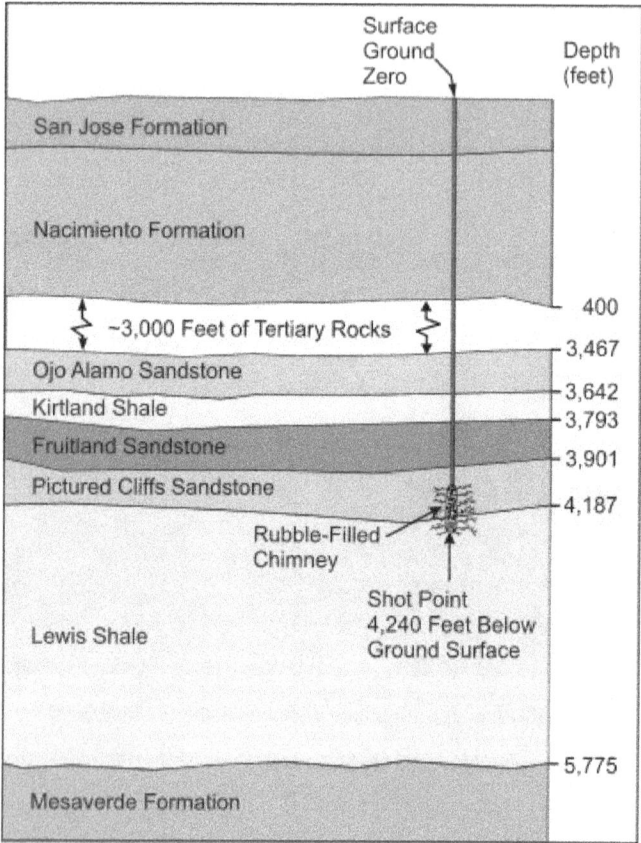

San Jose Formation

Nacimiento Formation

~3,000 Feet of Tertiary Rocks

Ojo Alamo Sandstone

Kirtland Shale

Fruitland Sandstone

Pictured Cliffs Sandstone

Rubble-Filled Chimney

Shot Point
4,240 Feet Below
Ground Surface

Lewis Shale

Mesaverde Formation

Surface
Ground
Zero

Depth
(feet)

400

3,467

3,642

3,793

3,901

4,187

5,775

Above: A US Govternment diagram for Project Gasbuggy.

"Gasbuggy Site Cross Section"
by Federal Government of the United States
Gasbuggy Fact Sheet.
Licensed under Public Domain via Wikimedia Commons

Hayawaka explains in the article how, in 1990, he worked with a visiting Japanese television crew to attempt to confirm the alleged existence of an "underground U.S./alien joint bio-lab" beneath Dulce. He also mentions that when interviewing locals, he and the Japanese TV crew were detained by the town's Police Chief, Hoyt Velarde, without any valid reason being given.

According to Hayawaka, Chief Velarde warned them, "Don't you ever ask any more questions regarding such a base. I have nothing to do with it and I do not want to talk about it!"

Hayawaka implies that Velarde's choice of words seemed to indicate the Dulce Base was known to the police.

Upon returning to Dulce in 2007 to investigate further, Hayawaka says, "...the son of the former head of the Dulce Police Department took me to the site of Project Gasbuggy.

"Project Gasbuggy was a rather 'strange' 1967 government project which involved a large underground nuclear explosion (29 kilotons of TNT) deep inside the high plateau area 25 miles south of Dulce, allegedly to release natural gas from deep under the ground. It was a joint project with El Paso Natural Gas Company.

"What is not frequently mentioned in association with this curious project was that the huge nuclear explosion had created, deep, huge underground extensive caverns all over the area along with extensive natural 'tunnels'."

In Chapter 9, we examine the strange case of American Philip Schneider who claimed to have been involved in a battle with aliens while he was working underground in the military base at Dulce.

Unsurprisingly, Dulce Base has featured regularly in popular culture, including an episode of *Conspiracy Theory with Jesse Ventura* titled *Ancient Aliens*, Pittacus Lore's bestselling young adult book series *The Lorien Legacies*, an episode of the History Channel program *UFO Hunters*, the 2012 video game *Ghost Recon: Future Soldier* and the comic series *The Invisibles* in which Dulce Base is shown to house a secret vaccine for AIDS.

9

■■■■■■■■■■■■■■■■■■■

THE CURIOUS CASE OF PHILIP SCHNEIDER

"I took care of John Fialla, who was best friends with Phil Schneider. How many people know about Phil Schneider? Well, they were using tunneling machines back in the mid-90s that could tunnel through a rock face at seven miles per day, that could cut through a rock face with high-energy impact lasers that could blow the nano-sized particles of rock so that there was no debris left, forming an obsidian-like core, and laying an inner core for unidirectional maglev trains that travel at Mach 2 to 2.8 underground between these very, very powerful and organized cities. There's 132 under the United States, an average of 5.36 to 7.24 cubic miles in size at an average of 1.5 to 4.5 miles underground, built, by and large, most of them in areas away from geotectonic areas – but there's going to be lots of new geotectonic faults established when you have force 11, 12, 13, 14 earthquakes hit the Earth. Why are they rushing to do this? Because they know that catastrophe is coming. And where's this money coming from? It's not coming from our regular Black Op budget. It's coming from the illegal sale of drugs. In the United States there's at least, by conservative estimates, a quarter of a trillion to a half a trillion of illegal drugs just sold in the United States that goes directly into underground budgets, and 90–95% goes to the DUMBs (Deep Underground Military Bases)."

–Dr. Bill Deagle MD, excerpt from a video lecture.

One of the most out-there, yet hard-to-dismiss testimonials supporting the existence of underground bases and the rumored ET's some of them hide, is that of American Philip Schneider (1947-1996).

Above: Film still of Philip Schneider giving a lecture.

(photo credit: public domain)

Above: Film still of Schneider shortly before he died.

Note the missing fingers!

(photo credit: public domain)

Although very few records exist on the man and his military career, Schneider stated he was a geologist and former government military engineer. Somewhat controversially, he also claimed to have been involved in a firefight that broke out with extra-terrestrials while he was building additions to the underground military base at Dulce, New Mexico, in 1979.

Schneider said he was one of only three survivors in the humans vs. aliens battle in which 66 US Delta Force soldiers were killed. Although Schneider survived, he had severe flesh wounds and burns to his entire body – wounds he claimed were the result of some kind of radiation weapon the ET's fired at him.

"A lot of the early nuclear 'tests' were actually attacks against underground and underwater alien bases, in other words."

–Phil Schneider

In the mid-1990's, Schneider began giving lectures all over the world about what he said was the absolute truth regarding ET's living below Earth's surface. During one such lecture, at the Preparedness Expo in November of 1995, he said, "Right now military technology is about 1200 years more advanced than public state technology."

During another lecture, Schneider mentioned how, in 1954, the Eisenhower Administration disregarded the Constitution by signing a treaty with the ET's. The treaty was apparently named *The 1954 Greada Treaty*. In the same lecture, he mentioned a human-looking alien who was "one of the aliens who has been working for the Pentagon for the last 58 years." He then produced a photograph of this supposed alien and showed it to the audience and the cameraman filming the lecture.

Providing a possible insight into the Splinter Civilization's monetary resources, Schneider claimed that since 1940's the US Government had spent almost *one quadrillion dollars* building hundreds of underground bases all over America.

"The Black Budget currently consumes $1.25 trillion per year. At least this amount is used in black programs, like those concerned with deep underground military bases. Presently, there are 129 deep underground military bases in the United States. They have been building these 129 bases day and night, unceasingly, since the early 1940's. Some of them were built even earlier than that. These bases are basically large cities underground connected by high-speed magneto-leviton

trains that have speeds up to Mach 2. Several books have been written about this activity ... The average depth of these bases is over a mile, and they again are basically whole cities underground. They all are between 2.66 and 4.25 cubic miles in size. They have laser-drilling machines that can drill a tunnel seven miles long in one day."

–Phil Schneider, from his final lecture, Deep Underground Military Bases and the Black Budget (1995).

In the course of delivering these lectures – some of which were filmed and are available for anyone to see on the Internet – Schneider displayed visible injuries, including missing fingers and chest wounds, which he claimed were a legacy of the battle with the ET's.

To back up his statements, Schneider also produced what he claimed were classified photographs, ancient alien fossils and non-Earth metal ores retrieved from Dulce Base.

In his last recorded lecture, Schneider told his audience there had been 13 murder attempts on his life by government agents intent on preventing him continuing to inform the public of the existence of ET's. He said he was speaking out because, "I love my country more than I love my own life."

Schneider was found dead in his apartment in Wilsonville, Oregon, on January 17, 1996, several days after he'd died.

As with everything else in Schneider's life, his death was also shrouded in mystery. Initially, the Clackamas County Coroner's office said he'd died of either a stroke or a heart attack. Then they changed their story to suicide.

It's also worth noting that all the geologist's documents relating to underground bases, as well as the alleged alien artifacts that he'd begun showing to audiences, went missing and have never been seen since.

"People involved with DUMBs, those courageous enough to risk being suicided— their leaked information suggests there are over 100 DUMBs ranging between 2.5 and 4.3 cubic miles, and two miles deep. The ultra-classified Black-Ops budget is supposedly 25% of America's gross national product (GNP), or about $1.25 trillion annually."

–Veterans Today, February 10, 2013 article Elite Underground.

Cynthia Drayer, Schneider's ex-wife, is one of many who firmly believe Schneider was murdered to prevent him leaking anything more about the ET-human interactions occurring below ground.

An interesting footnote to Philip Schneider's life is that he claimed his father, Oscar Schneider, revealed to him on his deathbed that he was not the German Jewish immigrant he'd always proclaimed to be, but was actually an ex-Nazi.

Schneider's father also apparently revealed he was a Paperclip scientist. Actually, make that a *pre*-Paperclip scientist as he was hustled in to America at the *start* of WW2 to conduct scientific research for the US Government long before Project Paperclip even existed.

Oscar Schneider went on to tell his son that as an American scientist he was involved in the Philadelphia Experiment. He also mentioned other exotic and clandestine government projects that may have included early underground bases, although Schneider couldn't be sure.

Schneider Junior said he was shocked his father revealed all this to him on his deathbed. By all accounts there wasn't time to compare both of their experiences before Schneider Senior died. Whether Oscar Schneider was in any way responsible for the top-secret military clearance levels his son attained or indeed whether Philip's own claims about working in underground bases are true, remain pure speculation and will probably never be proven or disproven.

"Phil Schneider, for example, who knew the facts and had directly interviewed aliens himself in Area 51. He knew what was going on. He attended underground UN meetings – the real meetings are not held in New York at the UN Plaza. The policy-making meetings are held in the underground military bases, what he called the DUMB ... He personally attended two of these meetings and said, after the second one, he was working for the wrong people. That was why he quit his service as a geologist for the government. He said it was run by aliens. He said that the aliens are in back of UN policy, and that they are in back of so many things that are happening on the Earth. He says that they are gradually taking over and are running, shall we say, "The New World Order."

–Al Bielek, from an interview by Kenneth Burke at the Global Sciences Congress, Daytona Beach, Florida in August 1997.

As one would expect, without undeniable evidence or absolute proof left behind to confirm Philip Schneider's story, there are as many skeptics as believers. The former include some who insist they've debunked all his claims about underground bases and ET's.

On the other hand, it could reasonably be argued undeniable evidence is exceedingly difficult to obtain when it comes to proving the Splinter Civilization exists and is in our midst.

The possibility that the builders of underground bases secretly promote outlandish (fake) alien stories as a distraction or a smokescreen must also be taken into account when it comes to assessing Schneider's story. On this note, it seems appropriate to end this chapter with reference to another quote from Norio Hayakawa's aforementioned official report of the Dulce Base Conference of 2009 in New Mexico.

"Hayakawa stated that he tends to support a theory that the government may have purposefully created some 'convenient' cover stories (underground alien base concept) to conceal those clandestine activities and may even have staged a series of fake 'UFO-type' incidents in the area, utilizing high tech equipment such as holographic projection devices *(and remotely controlled aerial platforms)*."

10

■■■■■■■■■■■■■■■■■■■

THE MONTAUK PROJECT

"It (Montauk) is very large. It extends for miles, especially the 5th and 6th levels. Almost all of it was constructed in the late 1920's or early 1930's. We talked to one of the men who was one of the contractors who built it. It was built on government orders right after the depression started. It was built in six levels. They covered the top over with earth. It's known locally as "the hill". It's a huge base. There may still be some use of it. Most of it is shut down. The power has been on for two years now, single phase 220 volt. The elevator used ran on three-phase 440 volts, and that has not been turned on, probably because they plugged all main

openings and the elevator shaft with
concrete."

*—Al Bielek and Preston Nichols, from an interview
titled Orion Technology and Other Secret Projects*

The abandoned Montauk Air Force Station
(aka Camp Hero) in Camp Hero State Park,
Montauk Point, Long Island, NY, has long been
the source of many an exotic conspiracy theory,
most of which usually involve underground
locations. For example, it's rumored that
Paperclip Nazi scientists worked at the
mysterious Long Island military facility
commonly known as *Montauk*.

The area takes its name from the region's
original inhabitants, the Montauk Indians, who,
according to the courts, no longer exist as a tribe
even though remaining Montauk tribal
members insist they do still exist. But that's a
whole other conspiracy theory!

Many independent researchers have
described Montauk as a secret research facility
where, so they claim, psy-ops like remote
viewing and time travel experiments took place
for decades before the site was eventually shut
down.

Some conspiracy theorists even say there was
a more advanced version of the infamous
Philadelphia Experiment conducted at

Above: Radar dish at Camp Hero State Park, Montauk, NY.

*"Camp hero radar ANFPS-35" by Nojo13 at English Wikipedia
Transferred from en.wikipedia to Commons.
Licensed under Public Domain via Wikimedia Commons*

Above: Montauk Manor – underground facilities below?

"Montauk Manor" by Beyond My Ken - Own work.
Licensed under GFDL via Wikimedia Commons

Montauk. You may recall the original experiment allegedly rendered a US Navy vessel invisible to enemy radar and listening devices – a story denied by the US Navy. These top-secret experiments were known as *the Montauk Project* and were reportedly carried out in nine subterranean levels beneath the abandoned Air Force station.

Quite a few Montauk Point locals have reported sightings of high-tech equipment being taken underground, and the existence of tunnels and subterranean bases throughout the region have long been rumored within the tightknit community.

In the 2010 TV documentary *Inside Secret Government Warehouses*, produced by the US cable network Syfy, the filmmakers went to Montauk to see if they could confirm the existence of underground facilities there. No tunnels or underground facilities were found.

However, ground-penetrating radar devices were also used and, although not completely conclusive, they appeared to show evidence pointing to some type of underground chamber directly below ground – a conclusion confirmed by the independent radar technicians operating the devices.

The TV crew also revealed a vast network of tunnels beneath nearby historic resort hotel Montauk Manor. Many commentators believe these tunnels lead directly to the Air Force station and were built as part of the mysterious Montauk Project.

"The last time two people went out there (to Montauk) to look they were abducted. They were knocked out electronically and taken underground to another facility where mental adjustments were made on them. They were returned to the spot, but one of them was not returned exactly at the same time as the other. There was about a 2 second gap and the one that was already there saw it. They knew immediately that something was wrong. They were given a warning. The underground system is still in operation. There are three entrances near AIL. They have three plants in the Farmingdale area. Brookhaven National Laboratories have an entrance to the system. There is also a connection to the Newark ITT Corporation building. From there a spur that goes to the ITT facility at Nutley. There is also a tunnel that goes from Newark to Wright Patterson AFB."

–Al Bielek and Preston Nichols, from an interview titled Orion Technology and Other Secret Projects

Over the years, numerous books have been written about Montauk and the Montauk Project. Among the more interesting is (the classic) *The Montauk Project: Experiments in Time*, by Preston Nichols and Peter Moon.

As the authors state, "The Montauk Project chronicles the most amazing and secretive research project in recorded history. Starting with the "Philadelphia Experiment"; of 1943, invisibility experiments were conducted aboard the USS Eldridge that resulted in full scale teleportation of the ship and crew. Forty years of massive research ensued, culminating in bizarre experiments at Montauk Point that actually tapped the powers of creation and manipulated time itself.

"The Montauk Project bridges the modalities of science with the most esoteric techniques ever imagined and finally catapults us to the threshold of the stars. We all know something is out there, but we're not sure exactly what."

The authors pull no punches in their search for the truth. This is acknowledged in the most recent (at the time of writing) review of the book on Amazon in which the reviewer states, "It took a lot of courage and perseverance to get this out into the public arena."

One who debunks the findings of Nichols and Moon, and indeed, all who speculate on rumored events at Montauk and Camp Hero, is columnist Oliver Peterson.

In an article published in the *Dan's Papers* newsletter dated June 5, 2014, Peterson writes, "Perhaps it was this early veil of secrecy that earned the base a reputation for much more than housing soldiers and protecting Montauk's vulnerable shores. Since the 1980s, conspiracies have circulated alleging that experiments in psychological warfare, teleportation and time travel occurred there and, some believe, continue at the site today."

Peterson continues, "Of course, as the Montauk Project conspiracy gained momentum and exposure, increasingly bizarre stories were added spanning all manner of sci-fi plot. Today there are hundreds of accounts, including child abductions and torture, extraterrestrial beings, inter-dimensional travel, Nazi scientists, UFOs, reptilian beings, a sasquatch-like beast and much more."

He concludes, "Whatever went on at Camp Hero, or didn't, or is still going on today, the decommissioned base remains a looming reminder of a bygone time and the Montauk that existed long before throngs of vacationers dotted her shores and development spread to every unprotected corner."

So there you have it. Polar opposite opinions on what may or may not have happened – or may still be happening today – in and around Camp Hero. Either way, even the most skeptical of us must concede there remain many unanswered questions concerning Project Montauk and its rumored underground bases.

11

■■■■■■■■■■■■■■■■■■■

OTHER RUMORED AND
CONFIRMED SITES

"Consider the case of three attractive psychiatric nurses, working together at the same psychiatric hospital, who decided to spend their summer vacation together in New Mexico. While enjoying the spectacular mountain scenery, they agreed to turn off the main roadway onto what appeared to be a short-cut to their destination, which was a health spa. Fearing they were lost after hours of driving, they stopped at a small store in the middle of nowhere. It was actually the entrance to an underground facility, camouflaged by an old storefront. Hypnosis revealed three matching descriptions of a large underground reptilian alien base. As the women left the store, they were disoriented, unable to speak properly, and barely able to reach their destination. One nurse sitting in the back seat was writhing in considerable back pain."

—Barbara Bartholic, from an interview in a 2007 edition of Karmapolis.

Cheyenne Mountain is NORAD's confirmed underground bunker at Colorado Springs, in Colorado. It was developed during the Cold War complete with missile defence systems and advanced space technologies, and is still in operation today.

The North American Aerospace Defense Command (NORAD) facility is basically a self-sustained city built inside the mountain. Some conspiracy theorists say tunnels extend from Cheyenne Mountain to other underground bases around the nation including Denver and Dulce Base.

Denver International Airport (DIA) is said to have an underground base concealed directly below its tarmac. Around the airport there are numerous fenced-in areas covered in barbed wire. To our eyes at least this seems a tad unusual even for an international airport.

Above: Former US Secretary of Defense Chuck Hagel (center)

in Cheyenne Mountain's vast underground base.
"Steve Rose, left, deputy director of the 721st Mission Support Group,
gives Secretary of Defense Chuck Hagel, center,
a tour of the underground tunnels of
Cheyenne Mountain Air Force Station
during a visit to 130628-D-NI589-130" by Glenn Fawcett
Licensed under Public Domain via Wikimedia Commons

Above: One of many bizarre murals in Denver's new airport

"Part of Peace and Harmony with Nature mural at Denver Airport"
by Mark Frauenfelder - https://www.flickr.com/photos/frauenfelder/7051540177.
Licensed under CC BY 2.0 via Wikimedia Commons

An article by the *North Star Report*, titled 'DEEP UNDERGROUND MILITARY BASES IN AMERICA', summarizes the suspicions surrounding DIA.

"There is the Deep Underground Military Base underneath Denver International Airport, which is over 22 miles in diameter and goes down over 8 levels. It's no coincidence that the CIA relocated the headquarters of its domestic division, which is responsible for operations in the United States, from the CIA's Langley headquarters to Denver. Constructed in 1995, the government and politicians were hell bent on building this airport in spite of it ending up vastly overbudget. Charges of corruption, constant construction company changes, and mass firings of teams once they had built a section of their work was reported so that no "one" group had any idea what the blueprint of the airport was. Not only did locals not want this airport built nor was it needed, but everything was done to make sure it was built despite that."

What's also strange about DIA is there are Masonic symbols everywhere, and freaky artwork depicting cities ablaze, women in coffins and dead babies adorning the airport's walls.

The same *North Star Report* article mentions the weird symbolism as well.

"Masonic symbols and bizarre artwork of dead babies, burning cities and women in coffins comprise an extensive mural as well as a time capsule - none of which is featured in the airport's web site section detailing the unique artwork throughout the building. DIA serves as a cover for the vast underground facilities that were built there. There are reports of electronic/magnetic vibrations which make some people sick and cause headaches in others. There are acres of fenced-in areas which have barbed wire pointing into the area as if to keep things in, and small concrete stacks that resemble mini-cooling towers rise out of the acres of nowhere to apparently vent underground levels. The underground facility is 88.3 square miles deep. Basically this Underground Base is 8 cities on top of each other! The holding capacity of such leviathanic bases is huge. These city-sized bases can hold millions and millions of people."

"Since the early 1960's, the American citizenry have been the unwitting victims of government fraud, perpetrated on a scale so vast that it staggers the imagination ... The total amount exceeds 40 trillion dollars ... The government has built an entirely new underground civilization ... In this new society, there is no poverty, no crime or

illicit drug use. In this new society, healthcare is affordable, energy is free, public transport is efficient. And you, the American tax payer have paid for it all."

–Dr. Steven J. Smith. Excerpt from the paper Underground Infrastructure – The missing forty trillion dollars.

Supposedly, there's also an underground base below the town of Kokomo, Indiana. For over a decade, Kokomo locals have reported hearing a hum coming from below ground – a hum so extreme some have become sick. It has even forced some residents to leave town.

Following numerous complaints, the mysterious humming sound has been formally investigated, but no likely cause has been revealed.

After living with the problem for many years and sharing information on the grapevine, many Kokomo locals now believe the hum is actually vibrations caused by machinery operating far below ground. This tallies with the beliefs of independent underground base researchers who insist large-scale subterranean excavations and tunneling are occurring beneath Kokomo.

Many have also claimed there's a vast underground complex beneath *Area 51*, in

Nevada, and that it also contains (perhaps literally) out-of-this-world technologies. The top secret Cold War test site adjoining Nellis Air Force Base, northwest of Las Vegas, has long been fodder for speculation the authorities have covered up reported sightings of UFO's and aliens. Until recently the government has denied its existence.

Now a newly declassified CIA document confirms the existence of Area 51. The document states the contentious zone was used as a testing range for the government's U-2 spy plane during the Cold War.

Mezhgorye is an enormous underground military facility in Russia's Ural Mountains, close to the city of Mezhgorye. The sprawling subterranean facility apparently required more than 10,000 workers to build it and spans over 400 miles! The military site has never been acknowledged by the Russian Government, or by the Soviet one before it. However, America received intelligence confirming its existence in 1992, according to an article *The New York Times* ran in 1996.

Some underground researchers believe the *Vatican* also holds subterranean secrets. And we're not speaking of the known basement areas like the Vatican empire's Necropolis or the Secret Archives, but rather an ancient network of tunnels, chambers and mysterious buildings miles beneath it.

Above: Area 51 – could there be underground facilities below?

Area 51 28 August 1968 / 7
Via Wikimedia Commons

Down in the hidden bowels of the sovereign Catholic state, bizarre ceremonies are said to be performed by Vatican cardinals, bishops and priests. Ceremonies which have nothing to do with Catholicism and everything to do with the religions of ancient Egypt and Babylon. But that, too, is a whole other conspiracy theory and something probably best left to bestselling author Dan Brown.

The mother of all underground bases may actually exist in the Southern Hemisphere. A subterranean facility known as *Pine Gap*, in the heart of Australia, is known about, yet not known about. Officially a joint defence and satellite tracking station, it has been reported by local media that nobody in the Australian Federal Parliament, not even the Prime Minister, has any meaningful information about the US-run base.

Local Outback residents have reported seeing massive quantities of food and supplies being delivered for what could be an enormous city below ground. Apparently, Pine Gap was constructed on top of the deepest drilling hole in Australia and is about five miles deep.

As mentioned earlier, in the late 1960's, one of us (Lance) worked underground at Mount Isa Mines in Queensland, Australia. At that time, it was roughly around two miles deep – and journeying by high-speed lift to the deepest level seemed to take forever. The thought of venturing five miles below ground is mind-blowing!

If Pine Gap is even half as deep as they say, it must be quite some facility.

12

■■■■■■■■■■■■■■■■■■■

BENEATH THE ICE

"There is in fact an underground base in Svalbard. It is the Svalbard Global Seed Vault. It lies 120 metres inside a sandstone mountain at Svalbard on Spitsbergen Island. Spitsbergen was considered ideal due to its lack of tectonic activity and its permafrost. It is 130 metres above sea level and locally mined coal provides power for refrigeration units. It is believed that the vault can preserve seeds for hundreds of years. The facility is managed by the Nordic Genetic Resource Center, but there are no permanent staff on-site. Norway, Sweden, Finland, Denmark, and Iceland began construction of the seed vault in 2006. It officially opened in

2008, and has a capacity to preserve 4.5 million samples."

—Michael Holtstrom, excerpt from essay on holtstrom.com

Assuming the engineering and infrastructure challenges are not insurmountable, Earth's North and South Poles would seem obvious places to site large underground facilities. Certainly, they're sufficiently isolated and therefore far removed from prying eyes.

In the Northern Hemisphere, above or near the Arctic Circle, the likes of Greenland, Iceland, Russia's Novaya Zemlya, Norway's Svalbard, Northern Canada and Alaska would seem to fit the bill; and in the Southern Hemisphere, Antarctica is as remote and even more underpopulated.

It's simply a question of whether humanity has the technology to construct massive facilities beneath the ice. Officially, the answer would probably be *No*. However, when you factor in suppressed technologies – such as those in the classified sectors of the military – then the answer is likely to be a resounding *Yes!*

Above: The United States' remote Thule Air Base in Greenland.

"Golf balls, Thule Air Base, Greenland".
Licensed under Public Domain via Wikimedia Commons

The enigmatic, mostly inhospitable and largely ice-covered landmass of Greenland is one of the most isolated and sparsely populated places in the world. It would seem to be an ideal place to build underground bases. And if there is a Splinter Civilization that has more advanced technologies than official science is aware of then the inhospitable Danish-governed country with a population of less than 60,000 people would seem to be one of the very best places this side of the Moon for safekeeping of such technologies. After all, Greenland has at various times throughout history been called a continent in itself and its landmass is similar in size to India or the entire Middle East.

Many investigators claim the US Military conducted a large-scale Cold War nuclear program beneath Greenland's surface. The ambitious program, which was apparently managed by the US Army, went by the codename *Project Iceworm* and involved the construction of a series of nuclear missile launch sites beneath the Greenland ice sheet and conveniently within striking distance of the Soviet Union.

These top-secret sites were apparently constructed under the ice so that the Danish Government would remain unaware of them as America did not have permission to build nuclear missile sites in Greenland.

As covered in the preceding chapters, the global elite have numerous underground bases – some of them confirmed despite being off-limits to non-military personnel or to anyone beneath the highest levels of government. That confirmation has usually come via reluctant acknowledgement from the Military Industrial Complex, tireless investigative reporting by a handful of brave journalists or, last but certainly not least, publication of declassified documents.

This accounts for those clandestine subterranean bases we now know of. However, there are persistent rumors that hundreds more such secret underground facilities exist around the world.

Many conspiracy theorists believe the US Army had, or still has, several underground cities – yes cities – beneath the Greenland ice sheet where all manner of secret technologies are being developed and maintained.

One of those underground sites whose existence has been confirmed is a former US Army facility in Greenland known as *Camp Century*, which was part of *Project Iceworm* and was also previously just a conspiracy theory. The Camp Century site beneath the Greenland ice sheet was selected by US Army engineers in May, 1959. Construction began in 1960 and it was soon a fully-fledged subterranean city that ran entirely on nuclear power.

Camp Century has long been declassified and is now an Arctic research facility. The US Army's activities there were officially abandoned in 1966, reportedly due to the unstable conditions that existed beneath the ice. However, given there was a B-52 nuclear incident in Thule, Greenland, that occurred only two years later, in 1968, a skeptic could be forgiven for linking it with Project Iceworm and also for wondering whether the project was actually axed.

Continuing with the Cold War theme, in an article headed *US Army's top secret Arctic city under the ice*, Curezon.org claims, "It eventually came out that the ultimate objective of Camp Century was of placing medium-range missiles under the ice – close enough to Moscow to strike targets within the Soviet Union".

Curezon also mentions a now declassified US Army film showing "the nuclear-powered construction process of Camp Century, beneath the ice of central Greenland".

The article continues: "Details of the missile base project were classified for decades, first coming to light in January 1997, when the Danish Foreign Policy Institute (DUPI) was asked by the Danish Parliament to research the history of nuclear weapons in Greenland during the Thulegate scandal.

"A report confirmed that the U.S. stockpiled nuclear weapons in Greenland until 1965, contradicting assurances by Danish foreign minister Niels Helveg Petersen that the weapons were in Greenland's airspace, but never on the ground. The DUPI report also revealed details of Project Iceworm, a hitherto secret United States Army plan to store up to 600 nuclear missiles under the Greenland ice cap...

"Danish workers involved in the clean-up operation claimed long-term health problems resulting from their exposure to the radiation".

Incidentally, the declassified US army film referred to in the article is freely available to watch online, having been uploaded to various video sites.

In the comments section beneath one such website that posted video footage of Camp Century, one viewer wrote, "The machinery and the whole project makes me think of the Thunderbird animations."

Who knows, maybe the underground facilities in the popular British science fiction TV series *Thunderbirds* were inspired by Camp Century or other similar confirmed or rumored subterranean bases of the global elite.

It's unlikely any of us will ever know how far the Splinter Civilization's rabbit holes extend beneath our feet. And whenever we see sprawling underground cities in sci-fi movies and television episodes, or read about them in novels, most of us still think, *This plot sounds far-fetched* or *The scientific concepts are ridiculous*. Right?

We'd be remiss not to add that quite a few well-known conspiracy theorists believe that senior Nazis built an undersea *colony* beneath Antarctica and even lived there after WW2 ended.

That base was supposedly at, or off, the coast of New Swabia, which was explored and claimed as a territory by Germany just before WW2 – in early 1939. The Antarctic region was named after that expedition's ship, the *Ms Schwabenland* and the Germans did state that their intention was to set up a base there. However, the region's official exploration is where the *facts* end and the (possibly fanciful) *theories* appear to begin.

One such theory insists that hundreds of Nazi flying saucers were stored in the New Swabia colony. Not only that but a secret *nuclear* war occurred there in the late 1980's between the US and the surviving Nazis, causing the ozone hole over the South Pole and "false" global warming issues!

As ridiculous as these theories all sound, the basic origins of this story may not be as instantly dismissible as you'd imagine.

Above: Did the Nazis build a secret Antarctic base?

(photo credit: public domain)

Above: An official Nazi emblem for their Antarctic expedition.

"Emblem "Deutsche Antarktische Expedition 1938 39"
by Deutsches Reich - [1].
Licensed under Public Domain via Wikimedia Commons

As ridiculous as these theories all sound, the basic origins of this story may not be as instantly dismissible as you'd imagine.

Could it actually be possible, that deep under Antarctica, the Nazis succeeded in building their base?

Before you call us crazy or shoot the messenger, consider the following:

On the July 10, 1945, just two months after WW2 ended and Germany had officially surrendered, a Nazi U-Boat was reported docking at a naval base in Argentina. At the time, a German submarine spotted deep in the Southern Hemisphere set off speculation about a secret base in nearby Antarctica. Was the U-Boat attempting the final relocation of the Nazi regime? Perhaps transporting senior SS officers to their freedom? Or was it simply a rogue U-Boat that had somehow ended up a long, long way from home?

Some 10,000 Nazis migrated to Argentina post-WW2. Officially, this was said to be because Argentina, like several other South American countries, welcomed Germans. However, could there have been a geographical reason for moving to Argentina, the southern-most country in the world? A country that extends very close to where Antarctica begins, let's not forget.

When a second German U-Boat docked in Argentina a month later in August 1945, the rumor-mill intensified. That same year, one Argentinean journalist, Ladislas Szabo, published a detailed article in leading newspaper *La Critica*, stating that Adolf Hitler hadn't committed suicide but was in fact in one of the two mysterious U-Boats that had arrived in the South American nation.

Szabo went on to state in the article that Hitler had relocated to NuSchwabenland in Antarctica – the original site for the pre-WW2 German base.

At the time, the Argentinian journalist's article was picked up by major newspapers around the world with headlines like "Hitler's on Ice in Antarctic".

Szabo continued to research the theory that Hitler was living in an underground base in Antarctica, eventually publishing a book titled *Hitler is Alive*. According to the journalist, the Nazi underground base under the ice in NuSchwabenland was "the size of a small city".

Independent researchers Colonel Howard A. Buechner and Captain Wilhelm Bernhart also investigated Szabo's story and concluded that by the mid-late 1940's (i.e. *after* WW2) German subs were bringing enough provisions to Antarctica to set up Hitler's refuge in the rumored underground "colony".

Admiral Donitz, a German naval commander who also served as the president of Germany for one month in 1945, told the Nuremberg trial that the Nazis had succeeded in building an "invulnerable fortress, a paradise-like oasis in the middle of eternal ice".

Admittedly, all the above is circumstantial evidence and there is certainly nothing remotely resembling a smoking gun to prove the Nazis did succeed in building an underground colony in Antarctica.

But then again, it cannot be disproven either...

13

■■■■■■■■■■■■■■■■■■■

UNDERSEA BASES

"The North Atlantic seems to be very significant and is possibly (the site of) the largest sea base in European waters. Other reported underwater bases are in South America waters – in the areas of Puerto Rico and Brazil – in Antarctica and other deep unobserved areas of ocean."

–Tony Dodd, former British police officer.

Could there also be secret military facilities under our ocean floors?

In 1969, the Stanford Research Institute in Menlo Park, California, published a report titled

The Feasibility of manned in-bottom bases. The report states, "The construction of thirty in-bottom bases within the ocean floors is technically and economically feasible ... The cost of such a base program would be about $2.7 billion".

Now keep in mind that was in 1969. So given the multi-trillion dollar black budgets numerous researchers claim the US Government and its agencies have access to annually, who is to say undersea bases weren't financed and built decades ago?

Interestingly, the Stanford Research Institute's 1969 report also states that deep submergence vehicles would need to be developed to build undersea bases. The following year it was announced Lockheed had launched deep sea vehicles with the necessary capabilities to do just that.

According to a lecture that independent researcher Dr. Richard Sauder gave at the Xcon 2004 conference, there could easily be US-built undersea bases in the Persian Gulf, the North Sea and the Gulf of Mexico.

Dr. Sauder, author of the 1996 book *Underground Bases and Tunnels: What is the Government Trying to Hide?*, also spoke of the US Navy's undersea test and research center off the coast of Andros Island, in the Bahamas. He speculated that this facility, which is known as

Above: NASA's Aquarius research lab on the ocean floor.

"Aquarius exterior (whole)" by NASA
Licensed under Public Domain via (Wikimedia) Commons

AUTEC (Atlantic Undersea Test and Evaluation Centre), could be a front for an undersea complex of secret bases.

On May 1, 2008, UK newspaper *The Telegraph* ran an article about China's underwater sea bases. The article, which contained satellite imagery of base openings on Hainan Island, China, states there's "a network of underground tunnels at the Sanya base on the southern tip of Hainan island". The article also states that the tunnels allow Chinese submarines to travel out into the ocean from the base completely undetected.

"Of even greater concern to the Pentagon," the article continues, "are massive tunnel entrances, estimated to be 60ft high, built into hillsides around the base ... While it has been known that China might be developing an underground base at Sanya, the pictures provide the first proof of the base's existence and the rapid progress made".

Although likely to be more complex and costly to build than bases beneath land, undersea bases would obviously provide even more secure hideaways for the Splinter Civilization to go about their business.

It's unlikely China and the US would be the only countries building undersea bases for their naval advancements and other purposes.

CONNECTING THE DOTS

■■■■■■■■■■■■■■■■■■■■■

In summary, we must concede we have no idea how many of the aforementioned underground, under-ice and undersea bases are real and how many are the figments of someone's fertile imagination.

Our research has revealed some of these bases, at least, are real (à la Mount Weather, Cheyenne Mountain and Pine Gap) and their existence is documented and officially acknowledged, but there's no proof those other sites – the rumored, unclassified, unacknowledged, underground *black sites* – exist.

Nor do we know the extent of activity in the known subterranean bases or whether extraterrestrials have been, or are still, present

– or even if ET's exist. Though we have our suspicions.

Anyone desperate enough to find out some truths could approach scientists, engineers and military personnel who have worked at confirmed underground bases and try to prize information out of them.

Investigators could also go to areas where subterranean bases are rumored to exist and use ground penetrating radar devices to see if manmade levels, structures and machinery show up below.

We would also like to know who might be ultimately responsible for keeping extensive underground facilities and/or entire cities, secret from the public and even from politicians. In America, the obvious answer would be the likes of the CIA and the upper echelons of the military. However, sometimes the obvious answer isn't the right one...

In a 2014 interview with host Sean Stone on the alternative views talk show *Buzzsaw*, one of the world's leading UFO investigators, Richard Dolan, brought up a fascinating idea about UFO reports that could equally apply to the interrelated subject of classified underground facilities. Essentially, Dolan's brainwave is that we may be looking at things all wrong by blaming governments and their intelligence agencies for covering up suppressed

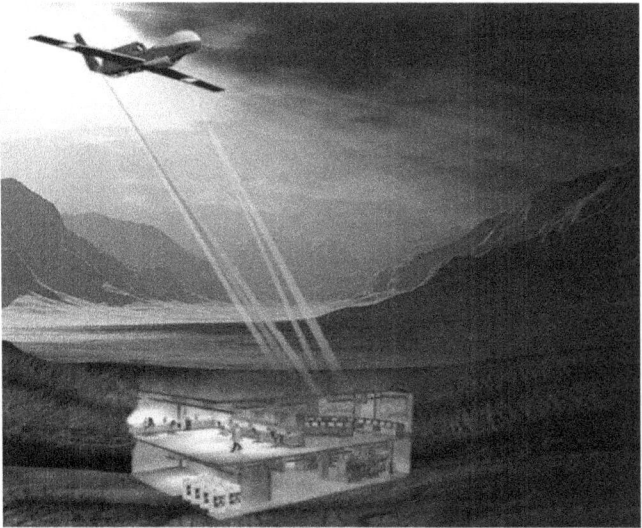

Above: A DARPA design for drones detecting underground facilities.

"Underground facility detection and characterization" by DARPA
This file was derived from:DARPA Strategic Plan (2009).pdf.
Licensed under Public Domain via Wikimedia Commons

"The way I think these things work," Dolan told Sean Stone, "is that the secret becomes privatized increasingly. And again I would emphasize for people to look at the general structure of the US military and to see how that has become privatized. And how secrecy itself has become privatized.

"In other words," Dolan continued, "if we were working in a black budget program, what are called special access programs, and let's say I was a Defense Department person and you were a person at Lockheed Martin ... You'd be the contractor and chances are you would have more power in the program than I would. The private contractors, as far as we can determine on these black budget programs, have the upper hand and they really run the show. The secret in other words is not so much classified as it is proprietary."

We agree with Dolan's contention that underground bases appear to have become increasingly, if not completely, privatized. Our research certainly points to that. If we are right, that makes unraveling the mysteries of secret underground facilities even more difficult.

Assuming it is true that certain scientific breakthroughs are kept from the masses by some kind of Splinter Civilization, it does seem highly likely, logical even, that some of these technologies would be stored in classified areas around the world, including and perhaps especially underground.

As we wrote in this book's intro, where else short of colonizing another planet could they hide the required plant, machinery and equipment – and the manpower to operate it – away from the prying eyes of Joe Citizen, investigative journalists and inquisitive everyday people like us?

Hopefully, we have given you something to ponder about the world literally beneath our feet!

OTHER BOOKS

■■■■■■■■■■■■■■■■■■

BY JAMES & LANCE MORCAN
PUBLISHED BY STERLING GATE BOOKS

NON-FICTION:

DEBUNKING HOLOCAUST DENIAL THEORIES: Two Non-Jews Affirm the Historicity of the Nazi Genocide

THE ORPHAN CONSPIRACIES: 29 Conspiracy Theories from The Orphan Trilogy

GENIUS INTELLIGENCE: Secret Techniques and Technologies to Increase IQ (The Underground Knowledge Series, #1)

ANTIGRAVITY PROPULSION: Human or Alien Technologies? (The Underground Knowledge Series, #2)

MEDICAL INDUSTRIAL COMPLEX: The $ickness Industry, Big Pharma and Suppressed Cures (The Underground Knowledge Series, #3)

THE CATCHER IN THE RYE ENIGMA: J.D. Salinger's Mind Control Triggering Device or a Coincidental Literary Obsession of Criminals? (The Underground Knowledge Series, #4)

INTERNATIONAL BANKSTER$: The Global Banking Elite Exposed and the Case for Restructuring Capitalism (The Underground Knowledge Series, #5)

BANKRUPTING THE THIRD WORLD: How the Global Elite Drown Poor Nations in a Sea of Debt (The Underground Knowledge Series, #6)

UNDERGROUND BASES: Subterranean Military Facilities and the Cities Beneath Our Feet (The Underground Knowledge Series, #7)

HISTORICAL FICTION:

Into the Americas (A novel based on a true story)

World Odyssey (The World Duology, #1)

Fiji: A Novel (The World Duology, #2)

White Spirit (A novel based on a true story)

THRILLERS:

The Ninth Orphan (The Orphan Trilogy, #1)

The Orphan Factory (The Orphan Trilogy, #2)

The Orphan Uprising (The Orphan Trilogy, #3)